September

K. C. KELLEY • BOB OSTROM

The Child's World

Published by The Child's World®
1980 Lookout Drive • Mankato, MN 56003-1705
800-599-READ • www.childsworld.com

Acknowledgments
The Child's World®: Mary Berendes, Publishing Director
The Design Lab: Design
Jody Jensen Shaffer: Editing and Fact-Checking

Photo credits
© Byjeng/Shutterstock.com: 6; Carrienelson/Dreamstime.com:
23 (middle); fstop123/iStock.com: 13 (bottom); Daniel Raustadt/
Dreamstime.com : 23 (top); GeorgiosArt/iStock.com: 20 (bottom);
Helga Esteb/Shutterstock.com: 22 (top); In Green/Shutterstock.
com: 13 (top); itsmejust/Shutterstock.com: 11 (top); Kim Nguyen/
Shutterstock.com: 11 (bottom); ktaylorg/iStock.com: 12 (bottom);
Library of Congress: 22 (bottom); National Archives: 19 (top);
Public Domain: 18; Samuel Borges Photography/Shutterstock.
com: 10; Shannon Fagan/Dreamstime.com: 20 (top); Spfotocz/
Dreamstime.com: 12 (top); Ukrphoto/Dreamstime.com: 23
(bottom); Yaroslav Sorokotyaga/Dreamstime.com:19 (bottom)

ISBN 9781626873735
LCCN 2014930712

Printed in the United States of America
Mankato, MN
July, 2014
PA02214

ABOUT THE AUTHOR

K.C. Kelley has written dozens of books for young readers on
everything from sports to nature to history. He was born in
January, loves April because that's when baseball begins, and
loves to take vacations in August!

ABOUT THE ILLUSTRATOR

Bob Ostrom has been illustrating books for twenty years.
A graduate of the New England School of Art & Design at
Suffolk University, Bob has worked for such companies as
Disney, Nickelodeon, and Cartoon Network. He lives in North
Carolina with his wife and three children.

Contents

WELCOME TO SEPTEMBER!

Goodbye summer, hello autumn! The days start getting shorter as autumn heads toward winter. Many schools start their years in September. Is this back-to-school time for you?

HOW DID SEPTEMBER GET ITS NAME?

In ancient Rome, the calendar used to have just ten months. In that calendar, September was the seventh month. *Septem* means "seven" in Latin. Later, two months were added to the calendar to make 12 months in a year, but September kept its old name!

A SAD DAY

September 11, 2001, was one of the saddest days in American history. Four airplanes were taken over by **terrorists**. They crashed all four planes. One hit the Pentagon in Washington. Another crashed in Pennsylvania. Two more struck the giant World Trade Center buildings in New York City. Both of those buildings collapsed. In all, nearly 3,000 people were killed.

Birthstone

Each month has a stone linked to it. People who have birthdays in that month call it their birthstone. For September, it's the sapphire.

SEPTEMBER AROUND THE WORLD

Here is the name of this month in other languages.

Chinese	Jiŭ yuè
Dutch	September
English	September
French	Septembre
German	der September
Italian	Settembre
Japanese	Kugatsu
Spanish	Septiembre
Swahili	Septemba

DISAPPEARING DAYS!

In 1752, England switched calendars. To do so, they had to make a "leap." As September 1 ended, the new day was September 14!

BIG SEPTEMBER HOLIDAYS

Labor Day, First Monday

Labor is another word for work. This holiday honors everyone who works for a living. It's always the first Monday in September. But the first Labor Day was on September 5, 1882— a Tuesday. Most people get the day off work. For many, it's seen as the end of summer— time to get back to work and back to school!

TALK LIKE A PIRATE DAY

Ahoy, matey! Arrr ye ready for this big day? Be ye able to talk like a pirate? On September 19, ye better be …or ye might walk the plank! A couple of goofy pals created this day. Now it's a craze once a year!

Constitution Day, September 17

The U.S. Constitution includes laws that made the United States. We still use the Constitution every day in our government and our country. September 17 is a day to celebrate the freedoms of the Constitution. It was signed by Congress on this day way back in 1787.

FOOTBALL SEASON

For millions of people, the end of summer is great news. That's because September and autumn mean the start of football season! Football is the most popular sport in America. Whether you watch high school, college, or pro football, it's time to start rooting for your favorite teams!

FUN SEPTEMBER DAYS

September has more ways to celebrate than just jumping into piles of leaves! Here are some of the unusual holidays you can enjoy in September:

September 6

Read a Book Day

First Sunday

National Grandparents' Day

September 12

National Video Games Day

September 13

National Peanut Day

September 15

Make-a-Hat
Day

September 21

International
Peace Day

Fourth Saturday
or Sunday

International
Rabbit Day

September 28

National Good
Neighbor Day

SEPTEMBER WEEKS AND MONTHS

Holidays don't just mean days…you can celebrate for a week, too! You can also have fun all month long. Find out more about these ways to enjoy September!

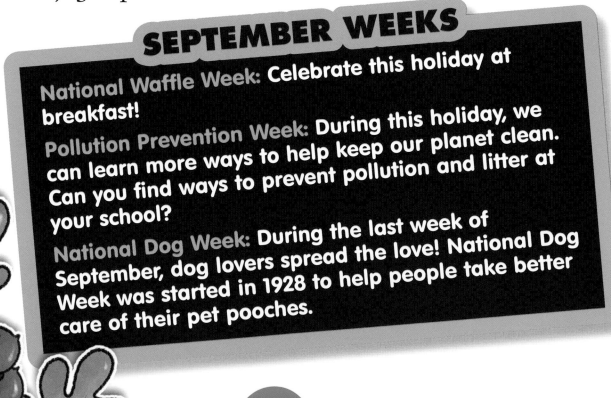

SEPTEMBER WEEKS

National Waffle Week: Celebrate this holiday at breakfast!

Pollution Prevention Week: During this holiday, we can learn more ways to help keep our planet clean. Can you find ways to prevent pollution and litter at your school?

National Dog Week: During the last week of September, dog lovers spread the love! National Dog Week was started in 1928 to help people take better care of their pet pooches.

SEPTEMBER MONTHS

National Hispanic Heritage Month: This "month" is shared! It runs from September 15 to October 15. Events celebrate how people from Spanish-speaking countries have helped make America. *¡Muchas gracias!*

National Be Kind to Editors and Writers Month: We think this is a very important month! But since you're all writers, too, it's be kind to everyone month!

National Honey Month: Guess how many flowers a bee has to visit to make a pound of honey? Would you believe two million? That's a lot of work. But it's worth it for this sweet stuff. Try it in tea, on toast, or on top of cereal!

National Chicken Month: Chicken is one of the most popular foods in the world. This month, tell your folks that many places have special prices for chicken. Try a new recipe! Have chicken every day!

SEPTEMBER AROUND THE WORLD

Countries around the world celebrate in September. Find these countries on the map and read about how people there have fun in September!

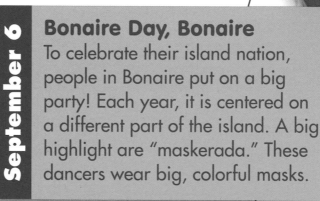

September 6

Bonaire Day, Bonaire
To celebrate their island nation, people in Bonaire put on a big party! Each year, it is centered on a different part of the island. A big highlight are "maskerada." These dancers wear big, colorful masks.

TINY COUNTRIES CELEBRATE!

Four of the world's smallest nations have national days this month. Monaco, inside southern France, celebrates Liberation Day on September 3. San Marino is surrounded by Italy. Its national day is September 3. Andorra is between France and Spain. On September 8, its people cheer for their freedom! Finally, Malta's Independence Day is September 21. Malta is an island in the Mediterranean Sea.

St. Wenceslas Day, Czech Republic

September 28

Wenceslas was a prince who ruled the Czechs more than 1,000 years ago. On this day in 935, he was killed by his brother. But people in his land still remember him for his great leadership.

The Birthday of Confucius

September 28

Confucius (kon-FYOO-shus) was a Chinese philosopher. He lived more than 2,500 years ago. Many people still follow his teachings. In China and Taiwan, they honor his birthday every year with ceremonies, prayers, and music.

SEPTEMBER IN HISTORY

September 1, 1939

By **invading** Poland, Germany started World War II in Europe.

September 2–6, 1666

The Great Fire of London destroyed more than 13,000 homes. London took years to rebuild to its original size.

REMEMBERING 1666

A huge tower in London stands as a monument to the 1666 fire. The marble tower stands 202 feet (61 meters) above Fish Street Hill in London.

September 3, 1783

The American Revolutionary War officially ended. England and the United States signed the **Treaty** of Paris on this day.

September 8, 1565

Spanish explorers created the first European settlement in the U.S. at St. Augustine, Florida.

September 13–14, 1814

Francis Scott Key wrote the poem "Star-Spangled Banner" after watching a battle at Fort McHenry in Maryland. The poem was later set to music.

September 16, 1620

The *Mayflower* left England, heading to America with the **Pilgrims** aboard.

September 21, 1949

The People's Republic of China was created.

September 26, 1580

Sir Francis Drake arrived in England by ship. He became the first person to sail around the world!

20

NEW STATE!

Only one state joined the United States in September. Do you live in California? If you do, then make sure and say, "Happy Birthday!" to your state.

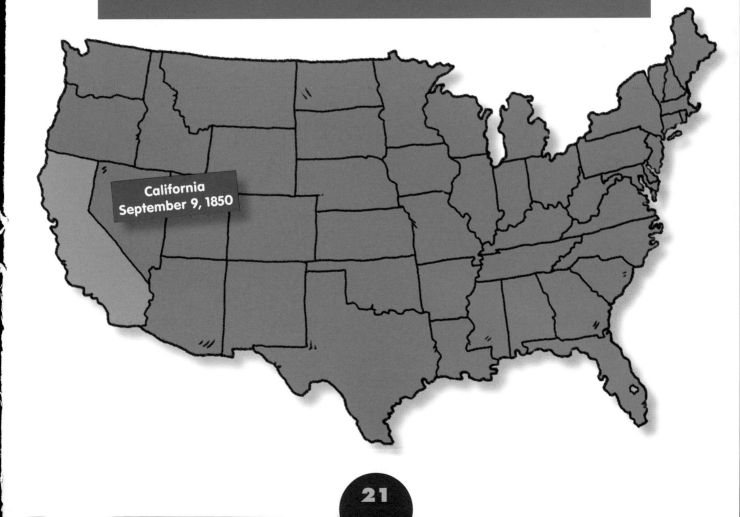

California
September 9, 1850

FAMOUS SEPTEMBER BIRTHDAYS

September 3

Shaun White
Light the candles for this snowboard and skateboard superstar!

September 5

Jesse James
In the mid-1800s, this legendary outlaw was feared throughout the West.

September 12

Jesse Owens
At the 1936 Berlin Olympics, Owens won a record four gold medals!

September 17

Jimmie Johnson
Johnson won his sixth NASCAR championship in 2013.

September 25

Will Smith
He's one of the world's biggest movie stars!

September 26

Serena Williams
The top women's tennis player in the world, she has been ranked World No.1 six separate times.

September 29

Calvin Johnson
This awesome NFL wide receiver has an awesome nickname, too: Megatron!

GLOSSARY

invading (in-VAY-ding) To send military into another country to take it over by force.

Pilgrim (PIL-grim) The Pilgrims were a group of people who left England for America around 1620.

terrorists (TAYR-ruh-tists) People who use violence and threats to scare people into doing what they want.

treaty (TREE-tee) An agreement between two countries.

INDEX

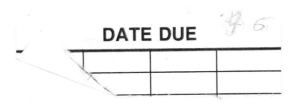